MIGRATION

Other Books by Michael Simms

The Longman Dictionary and Handbook of Poetry, with Jack Myers, 1985.
Notes on Continuing Light, 1980.

as editor

Dreams Crowded with Families, with Pamela Lange, Naomi Shihab Nye, and Cuyler Etheredge, 1981.

MIGRATION

MICHAEL SIMMS

BREITENBUSH BOOKS, INC.
PORTLAND, OREGON

First Printing: October 1985

Library of Congress Publication Data

   Simms, Michael, 1954-

    Migration.

    I. Title.
PS 3569.I479M5 1985   811'.54   85-3727

ISBN 0-932576-27-3 (cloth)
ISBN 0-932576-28-1 (paper)

Breitenbush Books, Inc.
P.O. Box 02137
Portland, OR 97202

Designed by Susan Applegate of Publishers Book Works, Inc.

Cover art by Laurie Levich and based upon an emblem detail from *The Belles Heures of Jean, Duke of Berry*, an illuminated medieval manuscript.

Manufactured in the U.S.A.

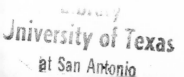

ACKNOWLEDGEMENTS

The author would like to thank the editors of the following magazines and anthologies where earlier versions of some of these poems first appeared:

Mid-American Review: "The Saying of Names"

Telescope: "Evening in the Adirondacks" and "Inner Ear"

West Branch: "Locating the Sparrow," "The Angels' Migration," and "Meditations in Galveston" (last section)

Touchstone: "A Harness, A Halo"

Bellingham Review: "Moon"

Intro 9: "On a Theme by Akhmatova"

Blue Buildings: "Duende," "Mutilated Prayer," and "Notes on Continuing Light"

Sleepy Tree Book I: "Enoch's Secret"

Southwest Review: "Aubade"

Espejo: "Violin"

The Rhetoric Review: "Freeing the Birds"

"The City" (formerly "Today I'll be Whoever I Want"), "Freeing the Birds," "Duende," "The Angels' Migration," "Gods," "Enoch's Secret," "Letter from Purgatory," "Mutilated Prayer," and "Notes on Continuing Light" appeared in a chapbook titled *Notes on Continuing Light* published by Blue Buildings.

The author would also like to thank the Yaddo Corporation and Kathleen Triplett for their assistance.

TABLE OF CONTENTS

The Saying of Names   1

Evening in the Adirondacks   2

Locating the Sparrow   3

A Harness, A Halo   4

Moon   5

Gods   6

On a Theme by Akhmatova   8

Inner Ear   9

Alba   10

Meditations in Galveston   11

Poem   12

The Explanation   13

Duende   14

The Angels' Migration   15

Depending on Words   16

Radical Light   24

Vessels   25

Enoch's Secret   26

The Ceremony   28

The City   29

Mutilated Prayer   30

The Blue Heron   32

Aubade   33

Dangerous Streets   34

Listening to the Radio   35

Midwife   36

The Sleeping Man   38

Top Hats   39

Letter from Purgatory   40

Violin   42

House of Rain   43

Freeing the Birds   45

Notes on Continuing Light   46

for Cassandra, Rebecca, and Christopher

THE SAYING OF NAMES

for Sandra Cisneros

Wild columbine, golden raintree,
　　　　wandering ivy, bridal wreath,
　　　　　　a woman crossing

and uncrossing her brown legs. She needs
　　　　a lot of love and so she hugs herself
　　　　　　as if a chill

has entered the warm room and sat next to her
　　　　like an old friend. Her name means
　　　　　　pink swan.

No one ever told her, she knew it
　　　　　　herself. Outside
　　　　the lawns that were green

then blonde, then buried under snow
　　　　　　are green again. She needs
　　　　the thought of this landscape

completing itself for her benefit,
　　　　the dahlias dabbing the air with a certain
　　　　　　　　ingenuity that urges

further embrace—the frugality
　　　　of a decision not yet made,
　　　　　　the bed,

the covers pulled up but the pillows
　　　　still askew, the lover closing
　　　　　　the door downstairs.

EVENING IN THE ADIRONDACKS

Always, it will be late summer in your mind:
birches give off a full and dark light

with a motion you know will abide and return
every evening. You are changed

by small things: an elm seed spins
to earth, and like your talent for the cello

the possibilities remain enclosed.
Being ordinary makes you a hero—

sweeping the porch, looking at the sky,
you become more than yourself. The solace for being

dull is being perfectly at ease with the world.
All afternoon

the afternoon sails in and out the window,
and the first star starts the lake singing.

LOCATING THE SPARROW

I know it's up there
in the golden tips of the afternoon pines:
the sparrow's single note
repeated insistently, as a child would chime

a glass with a spoon. I know
the movement of the branches and how the wind confuses
their shapes with the shapes
the mind produces

in its expectation of movement. My eyes follow
the jagged line of pines searching the source
of that sound separate
from other sources:

the yellow Volkswagen in a field
of dandelions, two boys leaning on the horn;
a repairman on a telephone pole,
his steel spike and hammer blows.

A pine tugs at the daytime moon
like a child with a balloon. I would climb
the pine to find that source that denies
everything but itself, a first love that defines

all other loves. The mind produces shapes
dependent on these pines,
the daytime moon, the field of dandelions,
the sounds of the horn,

the spike, the sparrow. On a sparrow-sized cone
the sparrow perches, its gray and brown body
disguised by the gray and brown shadows
pretending to be magenta.

A Harness, A Halo

He had grown tired of hurting, being hurt.
He had married himself, needing
no other.

She covers her body with a robe
of birds. While the bread bakes
she lectures him
on love.

We have to keep relearning our feelings,
she says, pointing to the swan
in his chest,
the swallow arcing over the laurels.

When mass stabilizes
it is called
weight.

When mass changes
it is said to have
radiance.

Look at the wild violets.
They've been a success in the backyard.

He notices the delicate
evaporations:
the eternal passage of souls.

He still wants only himself;
she her children—

a swan, a swallow,
a crowd clinging to a grain of sand,
each day like a harness,
each night wears a halo.

Moon

NEW

A dark melon sits on the table.
A knife slowly revolves.
When the edge turns toward us
the knife disappears.

HALF

Every night a blind man
re-invents the sky:
the whole city lit by a single bulb
at the top of the tenement stairs.

FULL

A white hat hangs on a black wall.
A big toe protrudes from a boot.
Inches from the clown's face
a cream pie stops in mid-air.

GODS

No sooner have we made plans
than love packs her bags
death snatches a friend
and the weather sours.
But even now, evening falling
like iron filings from the air,
nothing out the window but the clear cool moon,
we're looking upward, waiting for Gautama
the atheist promoted to divinity.

I was a stubborn sensible child,
scandalizing my family by refusing baptism,
not trusting my uncle, the country pastor
(frightful as God Himself in his black robe)
not to drown me in the blesséd waters.
How can I explain to them, love,
people invented death to give importance to their lives?
How can I explain the far shore we swim towards?
Mystery rebukes speech; silence swallows the syllables.
Death is simple as a raindrop falling in the ocean,
the ocean entering the raindrop.

I remember unwrapping the blue-barreled .22
on my thirteenth birthday.
A long lucky shot
pushed a crow off a bare-boned pine
in a deathward spiral
of black feathers among wet needles.
I remember the cat's heart in biology lab;
how still it was, thawing in my plastic-gloved hand.
I remember the mean red mare
slapped in the face with a bridle
until saltflowers bloomed between her eyes.
Somewhere a river of blood flows
drained from the flesh I've eaten
making violence swell in me like a burst fruit.

Remember Irwin Tuttie telling us his dream?

I'm hauled before a jury
of creatures I've wronged.
The Fly-God
judges me with indifferent eyes,
each eye large as a window,
each window open onto eternity.
The charges are read, sentence passed.
He reaches down
to pull off my arms.

———————

I know
when I die
I will evaporate
from my body
like sweat, like perfume.
Thin as a cloud,
heavy as rain
legislated by wind—
as happens now
lying beside you:
mists from adjoining valleys
mingle and become larger.

———————

The flat grasses sway, heavy with seeds.
The apple-light in the western valley fades.

These changes comfort you.
You think of death as one would think
of spending an evening alone:

shadows dissolve in the cool summer dark.
Your body becomes you.

On a Theme by Akhmatova

*I have enough teasures from the past
to last me . . .*

I have memorized
the shapes of certain faces,
hands lined with age and pain:

my mother sitting beside a dim lamp,
her face in the tired half-light
of middle age;

my grandfather holding
a silver watch to his ear,
his eyes rolled back
as if he were listening
to his own pulse.

A girl once showed me a scar
and told me how,
locked inside an asylum,
she threw a chair
at a mirror, picked up a shard
and opened her wrist.

My best friend's face
was calm as he told me
how his father's stomach rots:
year by year
the surgeons remove pieces
and put them in a glass jar
to show students
how slow death can be.

There are enough hands
clutching as I pass.

INNER EAR

In the silence of my room I hear
a faucet dripping, a fly beating

green wings against the window.
Two thousand miles from here

fishing boats return up an estuary
past houses scattered like dice.
You and your husband are

sitting on a black rock, quietly
discussing an unquiet divorce.

The mailman drops my letter in the slot
snapping the tightwire a spider made this morning.

Somewhere in Nepal
a snowflake lands on a mountaintop
and the whole mountain prepares to fall.

ALBA

I want to stay inside the moment
light completes the landscape

and everything waits
for you to decide.
A bird hangs from the sky,
suspended without flight.

The distance we've come
minding death.
I turn off the gnat-battered bulb.

If you are unquiet
you can reach far into stillness
and hear sheep grazing in mist.

MEDITATIONS IN GALVESTON

The salt wind lulls.
My boat is dragging
its iron shadow toward shore
where men cast and recast
their thin lines
into blood-colored pools
between the rocks.

———————

The woman I almost married
I think of now, descending
the luminous path
down the cliff to the sea.
The blue cliff of the sky
and the gulls
bringing in light.

———————

Nine-eyed, blue-blooded, helmet-shaped,
the horseshoe crab is not a crab,
but a type of spider.

———————

A seagull lights
on the balcony, examines
me examining him, and flies,
the motion continuous
and circular:
thought
moving into thought.

No alternative to sleep, just as
there's actually only one ocean.
The curtain swells
and falls. Gulls
and thoughts
of gulls
follow the same boat.

POEM

Far off I see,
as one sees a star rise in the waiting sky,
our unborn child
reaching out through you.

When you do something simple—
pet the cat, put on water for coffee—
I see in your distracted look
her face,
luminous, silent,
a generation unspoken, unspeakable.

We never named her, never
discussed the pain,
but a song rose to fill the world.

THE EXPLANATION

I think there is a likeness to all things.
The woods always seem to be waiting
for us to move on, so the trees
may resume their patient chemistry.

A painter friend tells me
he can't paint a tree
except by becoming one,
learning the activities of light.

I could study for years and never learn
what love teaches in a day.
My stepson shoots marbles.
His mind opens the fable:
what occurs once, occurs often.

The moon rises
in the transparent darkness, the air
filling with birds, the smell of pine and hay
and Christopher chants a line
measured by a poet fifty years before:
the moon, the moon is at the door.

DUENDE

Now I am going to create
a poetry that will flow like
blood from my cut wrists,
a poetry that has taken leave
of reality and reflects all
my love for things and
my amusement at things:
the love of death and
the joking with death.

—García Lorca
in a letter to Jorge Zalamea

You beat me with the silken straps
of your wings because
mercy makes me sick
and thinking about God
makes me dizzy. Torture, formerly
a melodious animal
inside me, has grown vicious,
a swan eating flowers from the aorta.

You teach me the tributaries of the Milky Way,
the bush of the month of May.
You draw your sword (*En garde, summer*)
and scare the cherries off the tree.
You convince me how ugly is the happiness
I want, how
beautiful the unhappiness I have.

As you leave, the animal
of my hand moves across the page.
Morning and evening change places
like acrobats in mid-air.
Come up slowly, crazy star,
I don't have your body:
my hips are draped in stone.

The Angels' Migration

Since no one collects the eggs anymore
soon there will be a population explosion
of angels. Some will starve,
some will knit shrouds
from the unanswerable prayers floating up,
but most will board leaky boats and arrive
like rain on a distant shore.

They'll live in tenements until they invent
the Angel Syndicate. They'll start small:
filching bedtime prayers, stealing the clink
of coins on a plate, helping themselves to holy water;
but someday they'll be twisting the arms of icons,
designing airplanes from pages
of the bible, extorting churches
for light filtered through stained glass.

The angels that stay honest will grow tired
of scrubbing halls where famous sinners
have walked, taking in nuns' habits
to wash, cooking stews of evening light
when the angels' own children
go to bed with only a story
of God's heavy boots in heaven's mud.

DEPENDING ON WORDS

a bird's nest fallen out of a tree
and the mother sparrow hops around
and around the broken eggs

Actions are born close at hand
and become visible far off.

———————————

Up the long roads of your heart
through Chiapas, Huehuetenango, Sonora,
you drove like a wind out of the Mexican hills
of your ancestors
and came to a woman laboring in her bed.

A fine skill we have:
we have delivered our secrets
and still have them.

Our well-built hearts
under the bone sky.
Stars call back to the crickets.

———————————

We wake in the cold before dawn,
feed and dress the children,
drive past the blank windows of the town
to your office where a farmer's wife waits, leaning
        on the porch rail, patient
        as a mare in her stall.

You lead her into the second-story sanctuary
where men and children are not allowed.
Rebecca sits on a stump and broods,
Christopher drops five smooth stones
        in a tomato sauce can
        and shakes it trembling
        like an ecstatic maraca player
        then stops, transfixed
by the spectacle of green rows of teenagers
        in an army convoy rumbling by.

Leaving the children in the fenced yard,
I climb the jumble of timber and rock behind the building.
From here, I can see the small houses of our many friends—
        carpenters and musicians—their many children,
the grandfather sycamore in our backyard,
white in late winter,
farms spread out like freshly ironed clothes.
I can see the black-glassed office
        of your slanderous competitors
        Midget, Miller, and Bailey,
and the hospital's green water tower
        misspelling in red spray paint
        Bubba's love for Irene.

Remember walking along the shore in the feverish
        moonlight—every shadow witness
        to our marriage of silence and work?
You were quiet in that garden of choices.

By now the *partera* is placing her hands,
        that were her great-grandmother's,
        exactly over the womb
and measures with her instruments of intuition
        the buddha-smile of the cervix,
        the strength of the double doors holding back the lake.

On the hill, the Ebeneezer Revival Church is alive
        with clapping hands and singing,
and over the lake, egret and heron turn
        in a blue flashing cloud.

———————

The weathered skull of the moon—
the ruined pear orchards.
I rise to go:
a mile of beach,
the sea wall.

———————

We clambered out the jetties past the sea wall
so Cassandra could take a picture
    of the pink granite striped with quartz and algae
    in the evening light of the last night together.
An old black couple sat on the rocks so close
    it was remarkable their lines didn't tangle.
Behind them, a bucket of fish they'd caught—
    whiting, sheepshead, shark.
The wife, her face smooth as the mist surrounding us,
    said nothing.
A tremendous tug on his line almost bent the rod in half.
He pulled up a huge whiting, luminescent in the last light,
and let me hold it up, while Cassandra took a picture.

My father was a gardener:
azaleas, pyracantha, the bloodberries, the thorns,
bay bushes giving off a sea of scent, applauding in the wind
jocasta, rose-petals floating in a still pool,
Ophelia's face repeated in a dream,
juniper, loblolly, post oak, live oak, water oak,
water maple planted in a creek bed,
tree and stream growing together; the stream grew
and shrank each year, the tree doubled in size each year.
Saturday his son worked beside him, building a rock garden.

The red wasp I've killed with a lunch pail
twitches its tail
in the green light of the greenhouse.

Christopher nudges the pretty needle with a stick
Rebecca asks what
is it now?

You remember how ill and confused I was
until I saw the horses on the white path.

A man may depend on words
and this may succeed
now and then.
The big rooster tries the night.

A heron calls in the shadows.

———————

The heron is not on the hilltop.
She is in the weed-shadows, minnowing in the still canal
calling her young *Moon-mocker*
and her young answer.

In the flooded marsh beside the highway
the egret lifts his beak, startles his wings
and praises the cow.

But what of the young stepfather late at night,
his new wife and children sleeping under the halo
of a mortgage,
a book open, unread, in his lap . . .

O teacher and butler who must earn love,
are you listening, listening?

———————

Pajaro bravo she called you
because you're always pissed off
about something. A machine
didn't deliver the poison,
so you kicked it in the stomach
until the police showed up.
Your wife locked you out because you were drunk
Open this door
No.
I'll kick it down
The hell you will.
The hell I will . . .

You bet your boots
the police are getting to know you
in this small Texas town
where women wear faces over their faces
and the best moment you've seen
was stepping out of the jailhouse on Saturday morning
with four dollars in your pocket
and a boy on a red bicycle raced you to the movies.

———————————

In the canebrakes beside the railroad track
a red-haired boy swings
a dead rat on a string.
A train passes. The earth shakes.

———————————

When a man and woman fight
a flock of harpies rises
from the blood they draw.

Filthy rapacious beasts
claw each other
in the foul air of the house.

Two people chained to a corpse
they drag through fields.

———————————

Heart, you've led me this far
        with your brouhahas
        and your glib carnivals of mind,
separating the yolk from the white of my sleep.

Now explain to me why
I have left my wife.
I'm taking a bus through a burned landscape.

———————————

Why is it that men are repulsed
by birth; oh they love the baby
and strut around as if they had made it
but from the blood and pain of the birth itself
they have to turn away

I think of the Chinese evergreen:
how wonderful to thrive
on too much water and not enough light.

———————

Death, my name is García-Simms—
half my wife's, half my own,
I traveled a long way on a bus.
Following me, you were disguised
as a gray woman hanging
her papersack baby
out the window, offering it to strangers.
Everything is yours
for the asking. It is you
who gently wakes my children
this plum-colored dawn, who dresses
my wife in her nurse's uniform.
It was you with your flashing forceps
who delivered me years ago today
into the plum-colored dawn,
and it was your ancient fingers,
priestess of Baal, that placed the inch
of placenta under the bleeding mother's tongue.
Tonight it will be
your toad croak accompanying
the small high singing
that blows out the candles,
and it will be you that opens the gift
and the gift will be you,
smiling, holding out your hand.

———————

We scrub the stalls
while the children play in the trees.
Rebecca dangling from a twig
yells *Look at me* and falls,
caught by her brother *Don't worry Mom*
I gots her

———————

We went to the park with the kids,
climbed the narrow shaft of the rocket
and blasted off
to the moon.

Alcohol: the thin whine of buzzsaws
in the right center of the brain.
Put the harmonica in the grass
so the wind can whip out a tune.

No, not the wind, it is
only the passing of our pale lives.

Strange to have someone in your body who is you
and not you, you said
six months into the journey.

———————

Rebecca is teaching me to sing
There was an old lady who swallowed a fly.
I can't do it. I can't carry the simplest tune.
All my life I've wanted to be somebody else.

Cassandra is teaching me to speak
Spanish. *I don't know why*
she swallowed a fly. Perhaps she'll die.
Que Quieres que te diga?

There was an old lady who swallowed
a bird. How absurd.
She swallowed the bird to catch the spider
that wriggled and wriggled and
jiggled inside her.

Are you listening?
All my life something's kept me from liking myself.
I give up.
I'll take lessons from a six-year-old and a twenty-
six-year-old to sing me
to love.
Myself. The dog that swallowed the cat.
Imagine that.

———————

Today the world was created.
The heron calls to its young
and its young answer.

Here you are, children, creators of light,
I am small.
I am the young husband
who finds terror in joy
as my children find fear in play.

———————

Half moon, blade of grass,
kite, diamond
ascend into the sky between two x's
cut by a little girl with scissors.

The Incas had a ritual:
"tying the sun"
when it went too far north.
In Machu Picchu
there is a stone altar in the shape
of a hitching post.

Radical Light

Birds wheel about the clock tower
as a storm moves in.
An old woman buries bulbs in her garden
across the street. Ninety-two
with thick brown hands and a nose for weather,
she sits on her heels like a crow
in the cold rain, the wind
flipping the leaves, flattening
the uncut bamboo. She works unseeing
staring into the gray wall of rain
until the sky turns white and holes of sunlight appear.
Then, as the bamboo rights itself,
a sheaf of light slides under the clouds
turning the stems red—the cowdroppings
in her hands are pink, decidedly pink.

VESSELS

A young woman, clay dust
clinging to her knees, brings a black box
into the gallery, places it under the skylight,
and wipes it clean like a mother preparing a crib.
She brings glazed pottery
fresh from the cool kiln.
She lights a cigarette, squints,
smoke curling toward the skylight.
She slides a vessel one inch out of shadow.
From the storage room abandoned mannequins
watch, the door ajar, a pile
of silver and black hands.

Enoch's Secret

Notice the moon and stars,
how they do not vary
their appointed
orbits,
how the winter trees
wither, except
the fourteen poplars in the yard.
The earth, so plainly
beautiful,
is held out to us as a gift,
but what do we trust
besides death—
the lantern in the body?

———————

What I saw in my sleep
I'll now say:

clouds invited me,
a mist surrounded me,
the stars and lightning
sped me, and the wind caused me to fly.

———————

The angel who had me by the arm said,
this place is the end
of heaven, a prison
for stars.
Those stars rolling
over the fire
failed
in the beginning of time
to come forth as they were appointed.

We came to four hollow places,
deep and smooth.
Three were dark, one bright,
a water fountain
in its midst.
I said, how smooth
are these hollow places
and deep and dark to view.

———————

Beside the fountain a dead man
made suit. I
asked Raphael the angel,
this spirit which makes suit
whose is it,
whose voice goes forth
and makes suit to heaven?

And Raphael answered,
Penemu taught men the bitter
and the sweet. He taught them
the secret of writing
whereby many
sinned
from time to time.

THE CEREMONY

We want to be
    surprised out of propriety
        without knowing how

    or why. We never
rise so high as when
    we don't know where we're going.

We exchange a glance with a passing
    stranger. We enter
a doorway and the soul travels outward

like a pebble thrown into a pond
    enlarging its circles
        to include the familiar.

We walk along the shore in the feverish
    moonlight—every shadow part of the ceremony,
        each thing exactly itself

until its secret is released—love
    refashions the world, nourishes
    our deciduous charms. A whirling bubble
    teaches us the mechanics of stars

    and the feel of the southwind
guides us into the painful kingdom of hope
    where music speaks of what we desire
    and shall never have.

THE CITY

There is a place,
a city old as memory
where azaleas line the boulevards
and the streets are named for saints.

Last night no moon, but a black sun
that sucked all the light from women I've known.
The alleys were lit by murders
and burglars slipped into windows:
may I never dream the murder I dream.

But this morning cherry blossoms blow into town.
In the marketplace a farmer lets loose
an avalanche of rutabagas.
A reasonably well-dressed man
cracks a whip, taming his heart like a wild beast.

A sidewalk savior, bloodpetals
blooming on his palms, rants
that the individual is the world.
This morning a regatta sails into the bay.
Doors fly open everywhere.

MUTILATED PRAYER

Men were created exactly like
the angels, to the intent
they should continue pure and righteous:
and death, which destroys
everything, could not have taken hold
of them, but through this
their knowledge they are perishing
and through this power
I am consumed . . .

The Book of Enoch

God's face flies quickly
always in the same direction
past the birthdays and never wasting
any fuel. The dream
continues past sleep and dies
      nude and alone.

On earth
God's eye is a rose
flaming in the pines of the sun.
The angels harvest ripe stars,
      toss them in the rolling barrel of thunder,
lift their skirts and hike up the steep clouds
      to the elegant embassy,
      its small mirrors.

———————

Stand up, sailor, geography lesson.
The sea wears a map of the sky on its back.
An angel is tangled in your sail.
A nightingale sings of the end of the world.
Save me, my zodiac,
I have lost the secret lines of my palms.
A mugshot of Judas is recognized
and an ensemble of denunciations
rises in the disordered air.
God wakes the heavens
with his crowing—
his delicate cruelties like a wind,
I would die of them
but for the special death
      that wishes me to live.

———————

Jesus, your three windmills no longer turn.
There's no saint to cure me.
Your rage has crushed the figs,
the centuries of women, the Jews.
I watch from the wings
your primadonna mother, the edifice
        of faith, the scarecrow of cherry wood,
        the mechanism of a rainbow
        in a scrap metal sky.

The moon listens at the door,
chalks the passover sign
and escapes. Now
all begins again,
all begins again, my god.

THE BLUE HERON

Beside the road leading here
I saw the bonehouse of a dead quail, askew
in its wings. Drunk
and lost in west Hell I'd stopped
in a taxidermist's shop
for directions. The only living thing there
pointed down the road
then tried to sell me you.

Rigid on a wire stand beside a stuffed fox
with a surprised look in his glass eye,
your ponderous wings extended,
your dorsal feathers too high,
your long legs dangling behind you like a rudder,
your minuscule head cocked,
you were locked in flight forever
ridiculous, grotesque.

But now, you stand on the cold shore, you sway.
Your cry starts low in your throat, rises
as you throw your head back, glides down the scale
as your head descends, the pitch
slipping upward with a lilt at the end.

Behind you, clouds gather above the promontory.
The light is like a great beached whale.
Seagulls slide by. Crows.
The seagulls blue in the blue levels of dawn.
The crows blue.
You stand in the salt shallows,
gaunt, motionless, quiet
where the tide washes minnows in.
A glimmer and you spear it, flip
the fish over and swallow it, headfirst.

AUBADE

The man lights the wood stove
puts on water for coffee, radio for news.
Sap in the split spruce boils.
The sun reaches through the window.

The woman climbs toward waking.
She dresses and slips into the kitchen
quiet as light. They hug
and stand together in the maturing morning
not sure where one ends and one begins.

Later he carries a bucket of ashes
to the road. The crows in the tall pines
warn of his trespass.
He fills a pothole and pauses

beside bare furrowed fields.
Steam rises from the remnants of snow
the dense hedgerow shadows—
it's hard to know exactly
where the ground ends and the air begins.

DANGEROUS STREETS

"I'm not a bad father really.
It's true I have a temper like a hammer
when I'm tired, and sometimes I'm thirsty
after the bars have closed
and I've walked dangerous streets
to get home and find she's drunk the beer
I was saving to silence the voice that screams stop.

"I guess I loved her too much to stop
because her face collapsed like a paper lantern
and I was her age swimming past the breakers
letting the tide carry me too far.
My breath turned to rock and I climbed
hand over hand toward a dozen moons staring down."

LISTENING TO THE RADIO

The love songs are interrupted.
The forecast predicts a hurricane
with a name that brings to mind a widow
with nothing to lose, coconut palms
bending over backwards to please her,
mudhuts and bridges returning their elements,
while the sea riffles its pages
like a diary reread for the last time.
A war is being born and already
teenagers march off to feed it.
The cities like drunken citizens
reel over the landscape and over
the cliff. And you and I
sipping our concoctions while we ponder
the steel ball of the September sky
ricocheting through space—what can we do
about these surveyors pounding the first red flags
where disaster's new freeway will be?
The hole is deep
and falling won't be much different
from sitting here, listening to the radio.

MIDWIFE

for Cassandra

I fall into the warm country.
You rise quietly:
I have to catch a baby.
Kissing me, the moon fills the road.

You wander the dark of the world
and at the harbor, a man in the gutter
sees you, kicks, tries to stand, falls away.

———————

Summoned to the waterfront tenement,
among the shacks heaped like overlapping bodies
You search for the fourteen-year-old illegal immigrant.

Her air is torn across.
Her breasts have turned transparent.
Someone is kicking his way out.
Her water bursts.
She looks down at the black hill
she has become.

———————

On the television, the breathless whine of Peter Lorre:

*I don't want to startle you, but
they are going to kill most of us.*

A butcher's holiday:
the dying were dragged off and others brought on.
I thought of the moon in a well
the whole time,
cries over the strange hill.

———————

The stars look down with idiot eyes.
The motion is accomplished:
the egret and the gull and the fisherman on the pier
and the many desperate beautiful arms about us.

———————

Somewhere at world's end,
supreme in the distance, veiled
by horizon clouds,
the ancient midwives stand:
blood on the water, light on a smooth stick.

The architecture of a newborn's cry.
Stone rain. Stone air.
Silt of destinies.

––––––––––––

The machinery of sleep turns its first wheel.

Someone standing in the harbor
early morning, full of peace,
might have heard a woman singing to her drowsy child.

Partera, sage femme,
do not hide your face.
I have seen apparitions before
in my sleep.

And the child is pushed into the world
butt-first,
giving up his doubleness, still joined:

a formidable light in the East.

In the junkyard, among rusting shells of automobiles,
headless dolls, rat-chewed magazines, bullet-riddled stop signs,
a mango tree blooms,
and beyond, iridium flowers on the sea surface.

Your vanity and desire vanish
and your thinking
joins the thinking of trees and wind,
the eye of the leaf, the thought of the wave,
the one creature which is everything.

THE SLEEPING MAN

flies without moving.
He caresses death
to wear it out.

Each feather costs
an enormous ransom,
but he profits from

the lie of its value.
His wife wants him
to change:

he had in mind
wings of smoke,
she grafts instead

wings of man.
He dreams of real pain.
His shoulders are aflame.

Top Hats

The white horse of the moon
is grazing in the fields.
The children are asleep.
You and I sweep the blue earth.
Poems I haven't seen in years stroll by
wearing top hats and swinging canes
as they sing. But you need more,
more than the ordinary wreckage
of the usual marriage. All we have
is the immense example of the sky
and at night the slow hard pull
toward something becoming known.

LETTER FROM PURGATORY

Dear Idiot, to you
I turn over the keys
of the town.
In the left drawer you'll find
my bones,
in the right memories.

Everyone I loved
was joined to the sky
by a rubberband,
while I had to support myself
or let myself fall.

Don't fool yourself
by looking at the stars.
How I wish you'd figure wrong
because of love.

The river sleeps in the shadow of the old
drowned one.

Will this landscape be signed someday?
Will I see a fox with a ribboned bonnet?
The red-lipped cowboy blue under the snow?
Will I see the apotheosis?
The situation demands it!

That's enough, America, you talk too much.
Tibet knows how to keep quiet.
Tibet knows how to play the flute.
Tibet knows how to walk above the earth.
She blinded her eyes and cut off her tongue.

I've had enough of things I believe in.
Afterall the earth is not
my country.
(May green-winged flies
suck the honey
from the flowers of her wound.)

[40]

To hell with it.
I'll give you something new:

the rainbow column of asparagus
is an eggshell
dangling on a string from
the Virgin.

O how you make me sick,
old incredulous
world.

There are people who go from Tibet
to the stars.
I tried to prevent it
in myself, but I'm poisoned.

I throw off my disgusting hair,
my nerves stretching
like a tree through my body,
my native land.

A pine snake, white
and red,
hangs his hat,
his coat, his little ankleboots
on the wild rosethorn.

A farmer finds in his field
the arms
of the Venus de Milo.

Wine splashes from all the drinking fountains.
Fortune rolls by our feet
(what do you expect, she isn't rich)
and we see
the golden firetrucks in their stalls.

VIOLIN

All night the sound of cats
wailing in the alleys.
Drunks threw bottles at the moon
and cursed because they missed.

Dawn has not yet peered
over the broken fences
of your sleep—
a winter bulb waiting to bloom.

———————

A moment ago, quivering
in my arms, you cried out
and your dream lifted us, carried us
like a wave carrying the drowned.

We breathe together:
two wings moving
in darkness, two hands
toward a diminishing flame.

HOUSE OF RAIN

Sky crowned with thorns,
swallows of the evening,
madcap runners,
the evening opens like a magazine.

And the heavens are so huge
you don't know where
to sit.

At night the traffic continues
on the streets of the ship
(I speak only of the streets and the runner
and his route across the lawns:
costly, abandoned).

Heavens of the evening,
you have the advertisement. You
have everything:
we naive poets envy
your scandals,
swallows, birds attached to petals.

———————————

Betrayed by its shadow
in a house of rain
a bird hides a head under a wing

    God hides under the bird
God tattoed with birds, even on his face

Does He sign his works
    with a lizard?

or with a storm?
        The sky has its stars
        The earth its whorehouses

———————————

Bicyclists and swallows,
        your river of love
            adorns

the bedroom window. Sunday morning
            the bicyclists wearing their
                    initials

                exchange bets. The gardener
                    sleeps on roses

in the sky. Runners
        ride the line of the horizon
                slipping away
            like a tuning fork cry.

FREEING THE BIRDS

From his studio window he can see
    the Berkshire mountains—closer
      a man and woman

at the evening end of their walk, and the fireflies
    tracing the day's
delineations. No one will interrupt him as long
    as he's here. So on the excuse
    of needing to work

he comes here and pulls his other needs
    around him. Right now writing
seems as silly as telling a bed a story,
    impossible as singing
    a radio to sleep. The day

darkens and the moon, which has been up there
    all afternoon, suddenly
    becomes important

    like a lover taken for granted. He has
nothing to say, but things are speaking
    through him. He repeats
    certain words, his tongue fluttering

over the syllables lined up
    like doves on a telephone wire:
    lassitude,

geranium, shrimp, cummerbund. He
    savors the definitions, watching
the alphabet fly off.

NOTES ON CONTINUING LIGHT

No one seems to notice the swelling I carry
like an insane mother her seed
to give birth—she thinks—to silence or pure void.

—Attila József

All night I've worked
imitating a certain great writer
while you slept,
the precision of dawn splitting earth and sky,
objects coming alive, separating.
Poplars take on shadows, move down the road.
Peaks emerge, covered with flowers and distances.
The road is rising and the fog is lifting.

———————

I will speak plainly, as you asked me to.
Everything I touch I give to you.
Everything you pass over in silence I name.

———————

Last night desire flashed over us like lightning.
We made love as if we knew
we would continue desiring
after we die.

———————

I've studied psychology but I can't escape the heart.
When the heart stops, something else—
perhaps the land—continues ticking.

———————

When I speak of the future
I'm following a scent in the wilderness,
while history hammers out iron flowers.

What are you storing up
that you smile in your sleep
like the wisest of dead pharoahs?

———————

When the machine of history locks in rust,
and the earth is liberated from its orbit,
the dead will assemble on the road,
transparent as glass.
I will stand before God,
and he will kiss my many faces,
and a crow will set out across cold space,
impenetrable silence.

———————

As you've noticed, America has not been herself lately:
she's been taking night courses in the mortuary arts,
waking every morning terrified of her clothes
saying *my body my body*
and her body doesn't answer.

———————

Soldiers fall in the hailstorm:
ripe fruit
no one, no one dares to collect.
Your daughter's white feet
cannot cross a sea of blood
unstained.

I return to you like a soldier
longing for peace
whether it was won or lost.

———————

As long as the world is crazy
I will continue to forgive myself.

Sometimes in my poems
I hold a small sick star up to the light.

———————

The October moon rolls across the sky.
The insomniac leaves continue to fall
on the raging boulevard
where a newsboy yells under a streetlight.
We hear it coming—the new century.
A train arrives like a separate little night.

———————

The mind like an undersea volcano
gives birth to an island.
Birds pass overhead, dropping seeds
of wonderful new plants,
and in the pandemonium of dawn
light unfolds like a frail auroral flower.

Our lost light returns.
The world does not know how much we love it.
Joy distorts everything in sight
and the earth itself is floating.

NOTES

The Book of Enoch is a Jewish apocalyptic text (circa 100 B.C.) that describes certain heavenly journeys of Enoch, who was the son of Jared and the father of Methuselah, and who was reputed to have never died. The book includes allegories and astronomical tables, as well as describing the hope of the occupants of Palestine for the re-establishment of the Jewish kingdom. According to the best scholars, it was originally written in Hebrew but is extant today in Ethiopic, Greek, and in Aramaic fragments. Sections two through five of the poem "Enoch's Secret" are adapted from the translation of R. H. Charles.